today and always
)but especially today(.

affirm yourself.
honor yourself.
love yourself.
treat yourself.
adorn yourself.
crown yourself.
find yourself.
balance yourself.
trust yourself.
grace yourself.
write yourself.
amuse yourself.
water yourself.
take care of yourself.

xo. adrian michael

love language.

love language.

adrian michael

a lovasté project
in partnership with hwttbtw
published by
creative genius
CONCORDHAUS

lovaste.com

Published by Creative Genius Publishing—
an imprint of lovasté

| Denver, CO | Concord, CA |

To contact the author:
    visit adrianmichaelgreen.com
To see more of the author's work:
    visit IG @adrianmichaelgreen
Book jacket designed by Adrian Michael Green

ISBN-13: 9798663985031

Printed in the United States of America

for lovers.

a playlist[*]

just right x raheem devaughn
all i do x shawn stockman
i like that x janelle monáe
go deep x janet jackson
chapter of the forest x trevor hall
closer x goapele
no ordinary love x sade
west x river tiber + daniel caesar
let's stay together x al green
vibin' out x fkj + (((O)))
room for you x joseph
do i move you x nina simone
love x jhené aiko
ready for love x india.irie
moon river x frank ocean
baby can i hold you x tracy chapman
gratitude x earth, wind, and fire
river x josh groban
remember x seinabo sey + jacob banks
holy x jamila woods
don't waste my time x usher + ella mai
heartbeats x josé gonzález
best part x daniel caesar + h.e.r
this ain't love x giveon
surrender x natalie taylor
is this love x bob marley

incense. palo santo.
tea. whiskey. wine. beer. water.

[*]*to be listened to, lit and sipped while reading or between readings for ultimate experience.*

ten things to always remember.

people make time for what matters to them.
sometimes you have to do the heavy lifting alone.
if you want to get things done wake up earlier.
all feelings are valid even if you don't understand.
if your impact is harmful the intention is void.
question why you're so quick to be defensive.
we're all suffering from something.
everyone deserves to be loved seen and affirmed.
you have so much more to give so give and give.
you never know who looks for and needs your light.

***

you never know who looks for and needs your light. that's not your style. you don't seek recognition and nor does light. you can't help but be sought after and emulated. so be you. you beautiful light. even at your lowest you shine bright.

the eleventh thing to always remember is that you won't always get it right or say the right thing or do the right thing but you can learn so long as you are willing. it isn't about being perfect it's about being heart. and when the heart is truly open that's when magic happens. and you beloved are beautiful magic.

what you deserve to feel.

appreciated.
affirmed.
adored.
assured.
abundant.

you are that familial feeling. deja vu. someone swears they have dreamed of you. seen you. witnessed you. felt you. somehow. someway. that's because you are everything they want in the universe. everything. everything.

***

you deserve a balance of all the good vibes and all the good offerings this world has to offer. that isn't hard to ask. you can do this for yourself but people need people. even if for a short while someone who doesn't really enjoy company wants some human interaction after awhile. may the ones you get even a sliver of your light make you feel appreciated. affirmed. adored. assured. abundant. because you are. don't let anyone take advantage of you. not anymore. that chapter has been done and closed.

you have been incredible since always.

watch how you grow
and see who comes
out of nowhere
acting like
they been down for you
the entire time; don't
get mad. give them passes
in the backrow
til they show you
they deserve
front seats.

you have been incredible since always. some people just don't know gems when they see them. forever amazing but there are people who lay in wait until you summit then show up to experience all your hard work. they can celebrate just make sure the view is from where they had you until you choose)you don't have to(to bring them closer.

your status has always always been gold gold. the priceless kind. can't even call it gold but that's the closest an explanation to compare the incomparable. this isn't ego talking. this is life. people will use you until they soar above you or squeeze you in order to get something from you. you don't deserve that. pay attention. they can still see you smile from the nosebleeds where they kept you at a distance since you been always trying to support or love or be there for them. this isn't a selfish flex. it's a warning and a reminder. not everyone is down for you down for you. but some won't give you the time of day until you become something or someone they can profit from. beware beloved.

it's not about finding the right words.

it's not about finding the right words. it's about opening yourself up and saying you don't know. like right now. there is so much going on. varied emotions. high anxiety. high uncertainty. many unknowns. lots of panic and fear. how to manage all of that. how to take care of yourself and be there for those you care about can be challenging if you look for the right answers. the right way forward. but what is more important is right now. being present. acknowledging. relating on a human level. on a heart level. to listen and be patient. kindness and much compassion is needed more than division. more than who you're voting for. so choose love. choose understanding. choose empathy.

empathy is a love language.
it says:

let me sit with you. and breathe with you. i may not know exactly what you are going through. but i recognize your hurting. your energy is depleted. it is clear)crystal clear(this isn't brand new. that this has happened over and over and over and over and over and while trying to heal you have had to carry the burden of convincing others to see your pain. know that i am not around just for the good times or the happy times or the celebrations. i am in this for the hardships. the lowest. the challenges. it is there where we grow. it is the place we embrace and get closer. i admit i've been too far away. never again. i'm here.

***

for too long some chose)unconsciously or consciously(to just show up for the goodships. not the hardships. they stuck by in the highs and vanished in the lows. but that can't be anymore. unacceptable. if they stick around just for the joys and deny you your right to express your pains then that is where the line is drawn. where you know their truth. your culture isn't monolithic. it is colorful and vibrant and rhythmic and blues. but if they don't love you for your blues then they can't fully love you. because you are everything beautiful and muse. everything necessary and everything worth battling for and with. no matter the tension. no matter the inconvenience. true empathy includes a full expression of seeing someone as they are and not just down to accept or tolerate or vibe in one breath and abhor and scoff and hate and ignore the other. everyone has their own needs but if it means denying someone else the ability to be their full self then that goes against basic laws of humanity. stay close to people who see you. and be the person you would want and need in times of difficulty. period.

the most beautiful apology
without saying i am sorry.

you said some things that made my heart ache. and for so long you've told me and told me and i said i was listening. but i wasn't. not really. my selfishness. my control. my fear. just said whatever i thought you wanted to hear so i could get out. to feel better. to pretend that your feelings mattered. but in reality my feelings were more important. my position. more important. my life. more important. but no more. and that sounds flat. empty. late. and you are right. so let me show you. sorry isn't deep enough. this is why my head heart and hands aren't present. you don't deserve anything but real change. real love. real effort. you deserve better from me.

***

you don't deserve anything but real change. real love. real effort. half anything is fake. and you aren't one to put up with anyone or anything that treats you less than magic.

ten beautiful things you should know.

you are wonderful. i miss you. you are my favorite everything. going through all of this with you is better than anything without you. there are too many too many's when i lose track of what to say. never for one second think you aren't the most important someone in my life. you make me better. you inspire flowers to bloom brighter. you are earth's muse. you make the stars blush.

***

no matter if your someone knows it you need to tell them. show it. bestow it. reassure them. keeping what is in your head and your heart doesn't always come out when you're not showing signs they can understand. open up. you'll be surprised when a sweet nothing becomes a sweet everything.

tell yourself. tell others. especially now. especially now.

it's okay if you're not okay.

it's okay if you're not okay. not feeling
your best. dealing with so much stress.
so much tension in your body. up late
and can't sleep. it's okay if you're not
all put together as you normally are.
but nothing is normal during these times.
you're going through a deep cleansing
and keeping it together really means
allowing yourself to fall apart and see
yourself in pieces. you're strong enough
to re-assemble yourself. you are your
own missing peace. relax your mind.
you are loved you are loved you are love.

***

when they care about your mental health they ask how you're doing
and don't accept just one word answers. you open and express
what's holding you hostage or keeping you joyous.

these times are hard being inside. but maybe it is time to go inside.
turn inward. and answer some questions your soul has been asking.

you are not alone.

expectations to remove from your mind.

you are deserving of a world that doesn't exist yet. to taste flavors of a love filled with ingredients that nourish you. but no one loves or gives or provides like you. nobody nobody. but there are some who will blow your mind if you give them a chance. you are hard to satisfy. how does one fill an already full moon.

***

you are the words wow in motion. but if you can let go of so many expectations it may just open up a whole new experience versus trying to control the outcome. they say expectation is a thief of joy and that has truth but you should know there are some expectations that are non-negotiable like. being around decent people who treat you right. wanting to feel special because you are. and people having the decency to be good human beings. not too hard to ask but sadly hard to come by. grateful people like you exist. reminds other humans to do better. i hope they lead by your loving example. until then. keep living and being a beacon for those that can't see and be as bright as you.

we need you.

go take deep breaths when and where you can today and write down three things you are grateful for. the first one you write should read: myself.

when to love more.

during hard times.
not on good terms times.
when it is too difficult
and not easy times.
at the lowest point
wanna give up times.
for love in those moments
multiplies
love infinity times.

***

you are loved not because you are easy but because you are there for the challenges. when it matters most. anyone can love temporarily but your love is forever.

love doesn't matter when it is easy. that is shallow love that soon fades. you deserve that deep water pitch black no bottom love. where you can't see where it ends and it just goes and goes and you learn from each other how to tread water. how to read the waves. how to hold your breath. and when it gets to be too much you go under under together. giving air no matter no matter. to the ocean floor and to the ocean surface. that's that love. that's lasting love.

how to apologize.

change your behavior.
don't expect forgiveness.
be sincere.

***

the ten commitments.

commit to love yourself during hard moments.
commit to breathe deep when you just want to run.
commit to clap for yourself when others do not.
commit to accept the parts of you seen and unseen.
commit to own your mistakes.
commit to take responsibility for your actions.
commit to choose you more often.
commit to open your heart and let others in.
commit to think and grow rich holistically.
commit to do your work and be a good person.

so much to recommit to. every day. every hour. every breath. the challenge is to be soft with yourself and be consistent with yourself to live with good intentions. you will hurt and offend and aggravate people along the way. the question is will you take the easy road and just walk on eggshells and keep the water still. or will you step lovingly and purposefully to make waves that shake and disrupt and unhinge parts of the world that need deep cleaning. no life is easy but no life deserves to be under constant attack. that isn't living that is surviving. and everyone deserves to live and thrive not fight fight fight fight and still end up dying with rage in their heart.

not responding is a response.

not responding
is a response.

***

i heard you. i noticed the messages. saw all the requests. but i'm choosing at this time to focus on other things. i can't give you my attention right now.

it's hard to be human these days. people want 24 hour access to you. they expect it from you. you can't think badly of them because it has been ingrained in us to expect instant responses. the moment i send you a text you better hit me back. and when i don't hear from you all the stories in our head builds up something that isn't real.

this is why boundaries are important. someone to tell you: hey, you can hit me up and that doesn't bother me but just so you know i'm not going to respond. hard to hear but there is clarity there. it's about them. and about you.

up to you how you navigate it but by not responding is a response. a mighty powerful one. to receive. to hold. and choose whether it is for now for later for never.

and if they don't respect it that is on them to figure out. you do not need to manage their emotions.

thirteen traits of attraction.

consistency.
light and passion.
kindness.
honesty.
generosity.
intellect.
respect.
gentleness.
growth.
vulnerability.
humor.
good energy.
beauty and creativity.

stay close to humans
who attract your soul.

***

there is something special about you. hard to piece everything out.
but people are drawn to you. like eyes to the stars. that something
something resonants and makes people feel like they trust you.
they call you home. they confide in you. they need to be by you.
there is something deep deep you may not even know. but it's
there. it's there. you're there. and that is a comfort. a peace. a love.
that cradles and rocks. you beloved soul are attractive. in ways
this language can't harness. so stay you. your heart is a necessary
remedy for souls in healing.

the brave way is to make waves.

the safe way is to float.
the brave way is to make waves.

i lose myself in the waters of others. we all do. some do it for seconds. the rest between minutes and their whole lives. eventually old air must be renewed and somewhere in that process a choice can be made. to float. or to make waves. to break free or to stay contained. we toggle in that space daily. may we find purpose in our own water.

***

i think about code switching. a lot. where in one space you act and speak and behave a particular way and in another space you act and speak and behave another. and in another. and in another. and how tiring that is. how toxic that is. how unhealthy that is. but for some of us we have no choice. we have to front. and hold our breath. and pull our hair back. and proper our tongue. and iron our tone. and make others more comfortable. to our demise. to our survival. code switching comes in different forms. we all do it in some capacity. some know you by your government name and some by your nick. some by street and some by intimacy. and when you transition from any of those spaces of knowing and not being known you can either be yourself or not. you armor up or you don't. you can be or not be. it's like entering the pools of others. you have to know their guidelines and rules and depths and policies and writtens and unwrittens and history and legacy and frequency and expectations and many times they could care less about your depths. your code. your heart. your language. your people. your goals. in their water you are theirs. to sink or to swim. and you agree to their terms. it be like that sometimes. but then it gets to be too tight. too unbearable. too unbreathable. and you're faced with a choice. to do it all again or to push back. to do it all again or to be your own pool. your own ocean. your own watered galaxy full of stars. the safe way is to float and that requires strategy and tragedy. the brave way is to make waves and that requires strategy and tragedy. and it's on you to figure out why. it's on you to sit with how. it's on you to recognize that there is magic and purpose and meaning and power and hallmark in your own water. in your own being. in your own image. they want you to think otherwise. break free. break free. be.

the kind of people to fall in love with.

fall in love with the kind of people who don't try to fix you. who listen. who aren't only interested in talking about their own problems.

***

everyone is a bit selfish but stick with the ones who genuinely care about you. who don't turn every conversation about them. keep the ones who you reach to who listen. attentively. sometimes with no advice but just two ears a shoulder and maybe some tissue. the best kind of love allows consideration. narcissists will make you feel like you don't matter. steer clear. fall and give your love to people who aren't hell-bent to fix you. you're good just the way you are.

miscommunication.

you gave me love
but not in the language
i needed.

***

you ever have nothing to say?

like your mind is blank. you are aware of what is going on but no words or thoughts come out. i'm experiencing this after two full days at a writing retreat. so i just wanted to share this insight. this line. this possibility. it came after a prompt about shielding. about denying. about shadow. we all do this. shield. we all run away from. so i stood in and wrote and wrote and recited and shared and there is still so much more down in the down there. these lines are about childhood. about formative years. about my mother. about my father. about manhood. about relationships. about self. about love. and the importance of being witnessed. this may not make any sense but i'm realizing more and more the importance of the pen. the importance of writing. the importance of retreating. to take time to self talk. to self check. to self love. to self compassion. and to really go where you have been shielding. to go where you're afraid. to go where you need. to just sit and just say simply i know you need me. i am here. i am here. i am listening. you are not alone. it is okay. it is okay. it is okay. and to return maybe not solved or healed or fixed. but better. but lighter. but freer. and to go back and do it again. so i ask you. what are you shielding yourself from? what is keeping you heart tied. mind tied. happy tied. what do you need to tell yourself. what do you need to hear. give yourself the language. give yourself the thing you need. it is liberating.

cast your bucket in your own ocean.

the terror is in witnessing so many people searching for someone to fill their bucket. they end up having to take out the waste and repair all the damage done by those who shouldn't have gotten close. but that is part of life. the cleaning up. bandaging wounds and learning. the mission isn't in knowing who to let in and who to keep out. the mission is to keep loving and leading with your heart wide open. to cast your bucket in your own oceans and your own galaxies and bump into people who don't see holes as flaws but holes as beauty marks. when you throw yourself out there you'll stand out. like them. wide eyed and so full. so powerful. so kind.

***

don't go chasing after what is most popular. and stop modeling yourself after people who aren't you. model yourself off of deep values that ground you. then build yourself in your own image. you'll get lost and eventually find yourself because you are on your own path and eventually this will be useful. so save this for that rainy day. all those buckets you need full you can fill yourself. but you have or you are or you will fill them with people who aren't good for you. or they are great and you tell yourself you don't deserve them or you're waiting for hardship or breakup to drop. but live and stay open. i'm at my time so i'm wrapping this note up. be yourself. and you'll realize too that other folks are trying to be like you.

three reasons people stay.

to be savored.
to be seen.
to be safe.

you do that for me. it is why
i stay. you are my here.

***

you have this way about you. that takes no nonsense. that calls it like it is. that accepts nothing short of what you deserve. and you care. and sometimes you pretend like you don't. but you do. your heart is too big to not care. but you're fed up with being taken advantage of. overlooked. because those with big hearts are the easiest targets. they let anyone in. they give too many do-overs. but that isn't your fault and it shouldn't be something to start putting bricks over. stay you. don't be like them. be like you. that's why people are drawn to you. the right ones always find the lighthouse. if you break yourself down how will those who need you see you. i fear that you're tired. burned out. fed up. aggravated. sad. disappointed. you have every right to be. but don't re-write your soul because someone stole your recipe. don't let them do that to you. keep showing up. and being. and smiling. and watching. and holding. and caring. and caring. and caring. this society needs your guidance. your people need them some you. i need some you.

anything that is not full love is fake.

accept love if it meets or exceeds expectations.
anything that is not full love is fake.

***

don't settle for positive attention when you know there is nothing under it. don't overvalue pretend love or else it diminishes and keeps you from what is real. it will cause you to question everyone after a pretender.

love is a love language
it says:

i care. deeply. deepest unseen. unsaid. shown.
the words i have for you sometimes get trapped
in my chest. the heaviness of what i feel for you
is intense)too intense(and when i see you my
whole body shakes. i want to be everything you
are to me. every part. every piece. every heart
space you fill in me i want to fill in you. you can
be fully you. all all all. no part of you should hide.
come to me. stay with me. look in my eyes. do you
see the water you create within me. lay and rest
and shake loose what you've carried so long.
drop it and be. no need to be anything other than
you. crack wide your soul dear lover. let me hold
you. you can let go with me. you are safe.

***

you deserve a love that tries its hardest to keep you. to help you. to hear you. to see you. to see you. to not try to make you anything you aren't already are. now is the time to show true love for those you say you love. the kind of love that saves lives. do what is in your power and dig deeper. don't run away. run to. fight grit sweat pry. hold on. if you don't receive this and give this then what is love even worth.

five things we all have in common.

the capacity to love.
the capacity to change.
the capacity to listen.
the capacity to influence.
the capacity to act.

may the power you have inside you be used for good. to unlearn toxic ways of being and decide what you thought was fine to ignore no longer is and become a champion for love and kindness.

***

there is so much greatness in you. so much potential in you. so much more in you. so love more. give more. say more. do more. care more. unlearn more. push more. dig more. think more. open more. you are already incredible and sometimes you don't know it.

a good person.

listens without judgement.
respects boundaries.
accepts others for who they are.

***

"understanding is the foundation of love." -- thich nhat hanh

today i get to begin again. to inch closer to personal goals and do what couldn't be done yesterday. today i won't be perfect but i will try to be more aware of what was beyond my awareness in the past. today is another chance to help someone. to help myself. to learn. to connect. to grow. to do less avoiding and more engaging. to be. to be. to be. a good person.

non-attachment.

let things come into your life and go out of your life without trying to hold onto them.

***

when we expect something to happen a certain way and it doesn't play out the way we wanted it to we get disappointed, let down, resentful, dismissive, sad, quiet, obnoxious, bratty, angry, a range of emotional responses can occur. when we detach ourselves from people, things, ideas, places, and objects we allow ourselves the opportunity to be less vulnerable to stressors, better relationships, feeling more in control, inner peace, improved health, self-confidence and being better parents/role models to the youth. non-attachment doesn't mean indifference or that you don't care. things still matter and you can still experience love and joy and passion and excitement. you're just freeing up space for non-judgement and clarity and ensuring no one has a hold on you that keeps you from moving and growing and experiencing and failing and learning and loving and having an abundant life. non-attachment is a process and not a destination. it helps when people come and go or if you so wish that a certain person likes you the way you like them. it releases you like a meditation that prompts you to notice thoughts and energies and sensations in your body and encourages you to spend some time there, thank the thoughts and energies and sensations and then carry on. non-attachment is a mind shift that may help you get through loss and hardship. not in the forgetting. but in the remembering and cherishing and gratitude for the memories and lessons and reminder that nothing and no one is permanent. sending you love wherever you are. xo.

the greatest relationship you will never have.

the greatest relationship you will never have
is with yourself if you continue ignoring you.

your two biggest challenges.

you care too much about what people think.
you apologize when they are in the wrong.

you're a good person and you have every right to stop
accommodating and start being firm and care more
about your sunlight.

***

sixteen beautiful things you should know.

you are someone's reason. their inspiration.
your voice is part of their healing ritual and
the dropping of any tension in their body.
your energy is contagious. you straighten backs
and draw the light out of others just by smiling hello.
you set the bar high for what true beauty looks like.
what goodness feels like. what courage sounds like.
you are the reminder and the model.
the action and the vision.
the glow of you is rhythm and blues.
you are sweet soul music love.

what a statement you are. what a statement you are.

i hope you embrace yourself more. and understand the fresh
air you are to so many. to so many. nobody else can do what
you do how you do where you do why you do the way you do.
even if they tried it's not from you so it doesn't feel the same.
what bravery is in you. thank you for being. you. thank. you.

seven ways to keep moving forward.

stop making excuses.
set goals and make a plan.
ask yourself why.
identify what's holding you back.
take the first step.
trust your process.
give yourself permission to fail.

heart and happiness.

one day you'll sync with someone who will always put you first.
who will choose to consistently care for your heart and happiness.

***

surround yourself with people who notice when your energy
is off and genuinely care enough to see why. to ask what you
need. to check to see how they can support you. too many
people out there carrying around heaviness in their souls.

you deserve a kind of love that knows exactly
what type of love you need.

if you ever wonder if you're enough.

if you ever wonder
if you're enough:

the universe is envious of you. you're mad enough and what they think doesn't matter. don't let self doubt ruin your worth.

***

one person too many is up wondering if they are enough. someone has made you believe something that is the furthest from the truth. but when you're constantly reminded of instances that cause you to doubt and second guess yourself how could you not feel this way? but the most beautiful truth that i know about you is that you're mixed with magic and human. built to be unique and not carbon copy of someone else. you)dope being(are worth a thousand heart opening affirmations times a galaxy. i know you're tired of wondering and i hope to put this to bed but even one thought of not being enough is nonsense. so rest, dear heart, put away negative talk. you're in a league of your own. of course you're not enough. you're way too much for anyone unable to appreciate soul like you.

when is the last time you said this to yourself.

i love you.
i'm proud of you.
look how far you've come.
i'm not them and that's my superpower.

don't be so quick to validate others and constantly ignore telling yourself what you deserve to hear.

***

there is nothing selfish about giving yourself the words you need to hear. if you detach your expectations of being seen or validated by others your overall happiness increases and you'll experience less disappointment.

stop comparing yourself to others.

stop comparing yourself to others.
stop comparing yourself to others.
stop comparing yourself to others.
stop comparing yourself to others.
stop comparing yourself to others.
stop comparing yourself to others.
stop comparing yourself to others.
stop comparing yourself to others.
stop comparing yourself to others.
stop comparing yourself to others.
stop comparing yourself to others.
stop comparing yourself to others.
stop comparing yourself to others.
stop comparing yourself to others.
stop comparing yourself to others.
stop comparing yourself to others.
stop comparing yourself to others.
stop comparing yourself to others.
stop comparing yourself to others.
stop comparing yourself to others.
stop comparing yourself to others.
stop comparing yourself to others.
stop comparing yourself to others.
stop comparing yourself to others.
stop comparing yourself to others.
stop comparing yourself to others.
stop comparing yourself to others.
stop comparing yourself to others.
stop comparing yourself to others.
stop comparing yourself to others.
stop comparing yourself to others.

five every day practices.

drink more water.
eat healthier.
protect your body.
protect your mind.
be aware of what you let in.

***

now is the time to be hyper aware of who and want you let into your mental space. physical space. emotional space. heart space. time space. body space. soul space. each moment can be a new start for this. no need to call it a cheat day and go back to old ways. be conscious about who and what you let in. it's more important now than it ever was. you get good at what you practice.

the practice of love.

you shouldn't just learn how to love someone or learn how to receive love through trial and error. the practice of love should be core in every space humans occupy.

***

love is a practice. love is subject matter. love is action. love is care. you deserve to be treated in a way that is considerate and nourishing. do the practical things. break from tradition when it means to do things better or take a chance on doing things different when the outcome has proven to not work.

you're one of a kind.

sometimes they will look for you in others
and they won't find you. you're one of a kind.

three agreements.

take nothing personally.
what's being said about you is untrue.
don't waste your energy on a little bit of rain.

***

choose your battles. people will always have something to say about you. that means you're doing something right. if you worry about what people think of you then you'll always be at war. let your actions speak for you.

seven admirable things about you.

you are remarkable.
you are phenomenal.
you are outstanding.
you are stunning.
you are worth staying up late to watch set.
you are worth waking up early to see rise.
you are full of wonder.

it's unforuntate if the one you're chasing doesn't vibe with you or notice how brilliant you are. because everything about you is admirable.

***

you deserve roses and someone to see
all the beautiful wonder that you are.

what to do when they leave.

hurt.
heal.
move on.

***

they were never there completely
they wait for
something someone somewhere
better;
but what they don't know
is that they will always chase phantoms.
i'm sorry they broke your heart.
rolling stones never find a home.
be willing to let go of what they
took from you.
hurt. heal. move on.
they did. you should, too.
difference is
they will always regret
their choice of
leaving you.

the best people.

those that put no restriction on what love looks like.
those that do not judge.
those that know others may have it worse than them.
those that make the world better just by being genuinely kind.

black lives matter is a love language.
it says:

witness. observe. take notice. listen to our cries.
we shouldn't have to prove or verify or plead or
convince you that the air in our lungs makes us
human. or the mahogany of our skin makes us
magic. or the rhythm in our bones makes us
beautiful. it doesn't mean black lives are
better or matter most or are superior.
it means get your hands off our
being. let us live fully and
remove all that fear from
your heart.

before you say "all lives matter". i'll ask you: what do you mean when you say that and why do you say that. do you want to be the center of attention. are you jealous. are you so badly wanting to have a poster with your identifier on it. what about a hashtag of a life that looked like loved like prayed like voted like schooled like played like you. do you really want to be in the news and other media sources constantly fighting for rights to be seen as a human being. do you want to live past 12 or 17 or 25. do you so badly want to be in a courtroom waiting to hear a verdict of guilty for someone who was meant to protect you but instead over and over and over and over and over and over and over it doesn't happen. tell me. do you want this life. this experience. this fight. or do you want to dance to it when it feels good but set it aside when the real fire starts. you still want to write in all caps huh. i figured. still not willing to let go of that power struggle. that desire for it not to be a reminder of your guilt and shame and deep seated hate of those who are needing to learn and plot and calculate how to get home every day safe and alive. black lives matter. shouldn't have to be an argument or a saying or an affirmation. it's a prayer that some of us have to seed into the souls of our little ones because there are those out there who don't think their lives matter. not enough to let 8 mins and 46 seconds to go by to let the air in our lungs slip away. if black lives matter offends you it should. go do something helpful to make sure we don't have to keep reminding you of the fear in your heart.

equity is a love language.
it says:

who isn't at the table. who is missing in this room.
where are our blindspots. what aren't we thinking about. there have
been barriers that have withheld and displaced and erased and
pushed to the margin the very people who built this place. whose
prints have been washed away to pretend they didn't have
anything to do with the riches that've been mined. open the door. no
handouts. or handups. unlock the bolts. what is it that will even the
playing field. that will close the gap of hundreds of years. all the laws
systems rules mindsets policies practices and so-called traditions that
intentionally deny human rights to the very humans who make this
world great. hate isn't the gold standard anymore.

we know it is impossible to treat everyone equally. it isn't possible. it is human nature to have some bias. some leanings. some favoritism. but it is possible to be fair and just and kind and aware and good. how dare people deny people to do things like vote when voting is our constitutional right. don't you see the game. call them out. people can't get away with modern day poll tax and literacy tests to keep the undeserving in powerful positions. if the word equity hurts your senses it's because you've always benefited from equitable treatment and don't want anyone else to.

bring your light with you.

frustrating. isn't it. knowing
who you are. waiting for them
to see your light.

***

bring your light with you.

you want someone that
deserves your strength.
not someone who makes
you feel weak.

nine parts of you to always protect.

protect your you.
protect your smile.
protect your fashion.
protect your magic.
protect your passion.
protect your space.
protect your heart.
protect your energy.
protect your love.

life is more fulfilling being authentic. when you protect your heart you're protecting all parts of you others tried to shatter and take. you aren't obligated to forfeit your self love. you are obligated to reinforce it.

***

protect your you. there is nothing selfish)ever selfish(about needing to keep yourself safe. to protect yourself from harm. too often people think this is self-serving and self-centered. it is. the most beautiful and positive thing you could ever do is to treat yourself gently and kind. don't apologize for protecting your soul.

beautiful is the soul that flutters.

beautiful is the soul that flutters
and inspires others to do the same.

to be clear.

if you leave me
when i'm broken,
you aren't worth
my time when i'm
whole.

on how not to take on their mess.

listen.
ask questions.
be a mirror.

it's not about you.
it's not about you.
it's not about you.

***

protect your heart.

gentle reminder.

you are everything that you need.
power up. dig deep. untapped magic
lives within.

it's okay

to have a bad mental health day.
to have a not so good day.
to have a hard time looking at yourself day.
to have a unsure how you feel day.
to have a not in the mood kind of day.

it's not okay

to define yourself off of one day. to be so critical that you judge yourself harshly and think you're not capable enough to be better. you are allowed moments of messiness and tangledness. it's about getting through not getting by. let your down days be when you love on yourself harder. give yourself grace. you are a beautiful human. remember that.

***

you had yourself a day. a week. maybe even a month or two or six. it's hard. and you're figuring it out. sometimes alone. sometimes you let others in. but you're carrying too many days as if they are part of your skin. part of your worry. part of your burden. letting them dictate who you are. let them go. all those days you couldn't get up. couldn't make a sound. couldn't feel a feeling. only thing you should be telling yourself is that those days made you more beautiful. more courageous. more human. be proud of sitting in the stuff that tries to tear you from yourself.

become the happiness you find.

document the times you are happiest.
notice what you are doing and who you are with.

this is your flow.
this is your zen.
this is your ma'at.
this is your path.

***

do what makes you happy and
become the happiness you find.

what i'd tell you if you left a toxic space.

it's hard. still caring.
but i'd rather see you
hurt and healing with
your heart intact and
not broken.

***

it's hard but you'll heal better.

oddyssey.

we are each on an odyssey searching for ourselves. and seeking true love in people, places, and other beautiful wild things.

***

cool runnings.

four let's to serve as remedy.

let breath teach you.
let sound bless you.
let touch soothe you.
let love heal you.

stay soft.

stay soft. and be strong if you must.
stay soft. and be loud if you need.
stay soft. and be hard when you must.
stay soft. and be firm if you need.

***

in a world that glorifies dichotomies and makes you choose extremes rather than understanding that we exist on a spectrum of being i say to you: stay soft; with a population of over 7.2 billion souls on this planet one must come to honor the beautiful cultures and differences rather than quip and deny humanity. i say to you, stay soft; we exert more energy into hating than taking moments to love. i say to you, stay soft; may there be a day that swords become plowshares and bombs become flowers. i say to you, stay soft. and in our softness may we see our individual and collective power, not in competition but in reverence.

let that comet inside of you roar.

be still. for a moment. dear heart.
let that comet inside of you roar
in place. for a moment. sweet heart.

***

become naked. spiritually. allow yourself to be. let the ocean that
swells in the middle of your soul and skin rise with the moon inside
you. give in to the journey. its peaks and valleys. you'll get where
you're going without compromising who you are.

fifteen stops to rid yourself of.

stop thinking everything is your fault.
stop holding onto toxic situations.
stop watering your inner critic.
stop avoiding difficult conversations.
stop pleasing people who don't deserve you.
stop doing things your heart isn't into.
stop hoping something will change without effort.
stop giving your attention to unworthy souls.
stop sweeping red flags under the rug.
stop keeping emotions bottled up tight.
stop biting your tongue for the comfort of others.
stop waiting to follow your passions and dreams.
stop drinking from the wells of poisonous people.
stop loving people better than you love yourself.
stop believing that you aren't enough.

you do the unthinkable. things only you would do. unselfish loving kindness is just the air you breathe. giving is a currency accepted everywhere. it's too bad you keep giving your precious energy to people unwilling to reciprocate.

you deserve more and it's okay to name it and stand behind it. no need to say it quietly. say it loud so people in the back can hear you. they heard you but now it's time they felt you. and if they decide not to move towards giving you what you deserve then when winter comes and they are cold they shouldn't worry where your heat is. you'll be long gone burning your fire elsewhere. and that isn't a threat. that's on your mental health.

as if love wasn't messy.

we may talk
as if love
wasn't messy
but in its fullness
it is chaotic
and has sharp edges
pricking and prodding
our insides
to remind us
it can be taken away
if forgotten.
love is
a beautiful
time bomb.

soak yourself in love.

soak yourself in love.

this is not for others.
this is for you.

the kind of love you've been waiting for.

whatever gives you peace. that's love.
whoever gives you peace. that's love.
wherever you give peace. that's love.
whenever you give peace. that's love.
however you give peace. that's love.

you can try as hard as you want to define and box
and point out the elements of love. of what and why
but you deserve a calm kind of intimacy. a calming
peaceful deep love that gives. that gives. that gives.

***

you are full of emotions and feel like you are scattered. most of us are. so just choose one thing. one moment. one to do. one joy. one whatever. and fixate on it. do it. you can't be everywhere or everything for everyone. but you can try to show up for yourself. to care for others. and know that is enough for today. then the next day you go down the list. or the next hour or the next block of time. be patient with yourself. be gentle with yourself. give yourself permission to be raggedy and messy sometimes. stop trying to carry all this expecting to be perfect. not possible. breathe. and breathe some more. you got this. we are in this. together.

ten signs you know you're growing.

you have wounds that are less tender.
you prioritize what should have been the priority.
you use tools you have learned to heal better.
you don't allow small stuff to get under your skin.
you ask for clarity before taking things personally.
you and your love language are being watered.
you are quicker to pause before you react.
you don't avoid talking about the hard stuff.
you think about what harmed you less and less.
you don't apologize for stating your needs.

you are a mirage and yet exceptionally real. the span of your authenticity speaks for you before words leave you. especially you. especially you. you are what is special and unbelievable. a big beautiful breath. what a fantasy you are. what a fantasy you are.

***

not everyone will be bells and whistles and celebrate you. or notice the incremental changes. the intentional work you've been breaking yourself for. patient with yourself for. pushing yourself for. no matter. you are doing this to be a better you. not to get the medal and stand for temporary applause. no this is deep work. soul work. hard work. life work. so when no one is there to see you hold faster and sit longer and breathe deeper and choose wiser and commit better you are there. you are the applause and the actor. the main and the audience. be proud of where you are. wine yourself. dine yourself. keep doing what you do. some will be waiting for your fall. but you. you will be there for it all. for the dips. for the rise. the rise. the rise. you are there for you. be proud of some you.

routine.

wake up in love.
breathe in love.

the light in you is yours.

the light in you is yours. everyone won't understand it. people will judge. gossip. curse. and ignore your existence. let them. you weren't born to seek approval. you were born to make an imprint.

you validate you.

five reminders you're royalty.

you are fierce.
you are strong.
you are spiritual.
you are humble.
you are human.
who knows
you're royalty.

you'll know when someone isn't good for you.

you'll know when someone isn't good for you when you let them into your world and there are negative side effects. you become ill. unhealthy. the moment you push them out and cleanse your environment you are whole again. healthy. well. the true test will be how often you let that same person)or type of person(into your life.

***

trust your senses.
allergies flare
around poisonous
people.

you made wings out of broken things.

you made wings
out of broken things
and rose above
the ones
that hurt you.

take care of your roots.

take care of your roots.

***

and be sure that whoever your roots latch onto help you grow. not hinder your growth. and just because what is above the surface looks nice and green. happy and smiley. isn't necesarily always the case. take care of your roots. don't forget to water underground just as much)if not more(than you water above ground.

never neglect your full self.

honor grief.

honor grief. sit in it. let it tell you where it hurts.

***

listen and learn how to heal yourself. your body will tell you what you need.

nine steps to recovery.

dress your wounds.
don't clean them with sorrow.
wash the pain with salt.
turn your scars into honey.
drizzle the sweet sadness into a hole.
cover it up.
walk away.
let go.
move on.

be the kind of human you'd want to fall in love with.

be the kind of human you'd want to fall in love with.

love is a coal mine.

courage, dear heart.
love is a coal mine.

***

your lungs may become full of soot. and it will sometimes become hard to breathe. just promise yourself to never stop singing. never stop singing.

vengeance is in finding happiness.

vengeance is in finding happiness.
not in waging war.

bloom into your own kind of beautiful.

bloom.
bloom often.
bloom abundantly.
bloom into your own kind of beautiful.

love is like water.

love is like water.
powerful enough to drown you.
soft enough to cleanse you.
deep enough to save you.

homeland.

you are your own homeland.
make pilgrimage within.

learn to accept or learn to suffer.

learn to accept. or learn to suffer.
you choose.

eight steps on how to replant yourself.

step one. add water. lightly water yourself to help the soul and soil slide more easily out of the earth.

step two. gently remove yourself from the current environment.

step three. prune excess roots.

step four. if you have outgrown current area. honor old environment. then clean and sage fresh new soil.

step five. replant yourself.

step six. fill in with more nutrient rich soil until firmly positioned.

step seven. water yourself.

step eight. grow.

six mindsets.

lose yourself in yourself.
adjust your mindset.
watch how things change.
be the love you wish to feel.
be the power you want to have.
be the greatest at what you already are.

***

you are the key that drives being. you are the shift.
just change gears.

ten crucial choices to make more of.

choose rest.
choose hope.
choose love.
choose joy.
choose courage.
choose resistance.
choose kindness.
choose compassion.
choose vulnerability.
choose you.

because when you choose you more often you give yourself
permission to be the best version you wouldn't be able to be if you
keep forgetting you deserve your deep love, too.

six chances.

1. bring up what you need.
2. remind them of what you need.
3. ask them for what you need.
4. demand for what you need.
5. far too many times given already.
6. protect your heart and walk away.

***

we all have unmet needs. but there are basic needs in relationships that you shouldn't negotiate or set aside when it comes to boundaries or love language or even minding your tone so not to get triggered. whatever it is. i say give someone six chances before you have to do what you have to do to protect your peace and your heart. bringing it up once just isn't enough. 100 times seems like you might be talking to a brick wall. six felt like a sweet spot.

every relationship is different and has various issues that can be worked through. but you know what you deserve. and if you can't even get the bare minimum how can you expect anything more.

four ways to express meaningful love.

pay attention to the details. ask about a specific project or say the name of a loved one or check-in about a recent worry they shared with you.

meet them where they are. notice the energy they bring to a conversation. if they seem distracted or short with you talk less in regards to you and center them.

establish loving agreements. commit to find common ground and language that anchors your relationship for moments that are easy and challenging.

wonder how. how is your heart. how can we connect. how are you healing. wonder deepens loving intimacy.

doing nothing is doing something.

doing nothing *is* doing something.
sometimes you just have to stop
)really stop(and consider what's
at play. if you want to give energy.
if you have the energy.

the choice is yours. the choice is always yours.

ten beautiful things you should know.

you are wonderful. i miss you. you are my favorite everything. going through all of this with you is better than anything without you. there are too many too many's when i lose track of what to say. never for one second think you aren't the most important someone in my life. you make me better. you inspire flowers to bloom brighter. you are earth's muse. you make the stars blush.

***

no matter if your someone knows it you need to tell them. show it. bestow it. reassure them. keeping what is in your head and your heart doesn't always come out when you're not showing signs they can understand. open up. you'll be surprised what a sweet nothing becomes a sweet everything.

tell yourself. tell others. especially now. especially now.

you will always grow wherever you are planted.

you will always grow wherever you are planted.

***

no matter the circumstance. wherever you end up.
through happiness and hardship.

choose to be yourself.

becoming magic is never easy.
but you do it everyday when
you choose to be yourself.

love is a painful thing but not always.

love is a painful thing. but not always.
there are moments when it is beautiful
and segments when it is dreadful.
sometimes a person is all you think about
and often furthest from your mind.
the secret is in the staying on the rollercoaster
both deciding not to get off.

***

one moment you're talking for hours. missing classes. daydreaming through meetings. gchatting)is that still a thing(all day getting no work done. spending every free moment on top of one another forgetting which limb belongs to which. and then something happens when that chemistry fades. not entirely but like you slowly sunk back to earth. and then you see all the little things that now get under your skin. the quirks and the pieces that you want them to stop. and then you argue and it gets harder and someone)or both(want out. distance happens then you're right back to how things started. and sometimes it is accordion like. up and down like a rollercoaster ride. but you stay. you stay. you fight. you pray. highs and lows happen. good years. bad months. hard fall. beautiful winter. average summer. love is a painful thing. but not always. you just have to remember to smile and laugh at the times that felt red but turned into yellow hues. stay in there. love is there. love is always there.

come with me.

three magic words
parted from lips

tells the heart
i want you
i trust you
you feel like home.

every part of you is magic.

every part of you is magic.
you feel like buried treasure.

***

stay close to people that remind of you this.

ten trust statements to take wherever you go.

trust your intuition.
trust what is for you won't miss you.
trust yourself when doubt creeps in.
trust that things will get better.
trust failure as a set up for greater success.
trust your heart even when you can't hear it beat.
trust any decision you make because you made it.
trust you are missed in every space you're not in.
trust your love to be the best love ever given.
trust you are always blooming. always blooming.

you are always blooming. always in bloom. always in process.
always working on and growing. you make your own weather and
that is what true lovers do. stay blooming. stay blooming.

five reminders.

you are doing the best you can.
you are not alone.
it's okay to ask for help.
it's okay to be sad.
you are a badass.

***

stop. right now. grab a pen)if you don't already have one(and spend the next five minutes writing down beautiful positive affirmations in the space below above in the margins on this page the next page any open space you can find.

the best type of happiness.

the best type of happiness rests
in small places. in the tiniest less
obvious spaces. you miss it if you
look too hard. you lose it when
you doubt you have it or compare
what you have found to the tide
of others. the best type of happiness
is when you can see your own water.
feel its powerful depth and proclaim:
i am enough. i am enough.

***

there are several types of happiness. if you inventory them it comes
down to joy, excitement, gratitude, pride, optimism, contentment,
and love. but sometimes you can't name that. and sometimes
it feels like happiness isn't attainable. especially right now.
but if you zoom inward and just slow down your mind and
disconnect from the heavy of this just for a moment)even if just
two minutes(there is glimmer of light and happiness. there there.
you just need to breathe life into it. into you. instant gratification
feels nice. likes feel nice. comments feel nice. but they go away. what
lasts is the energy and relationship you build with one another.
genuinely. find those people authentically if you're using social
media. connect don't exploit. people actually need something to
latch onto that feels real and honest and loving. the best type of
happiness is you. has always been you. always. always. always. tho
your water is expansive water can't see itself. so you must believe
in what you are and who you are and trust you're doing the
greatest that you can. because you are great love. the greatest love.

five pillow talk questions.

what do you remember about our first kiss?
what did you think when you first saw me?
what are you holding onto that i can carry?
what are you most proud of and afraid of?
what part of us needs watering?

ask and grow deep.

what books are you reading?
what made you cry recently?
what is your biggest fear?
what brings you joy?
what do you miss from childhood?
what do you dream about?

two signs a person is revolutionary.

they deeply care about people.
they know what it's like to be misunderstood.

a toast to friendship.

one day you will realize that the friendship you had always hoped for happened at the time you really needed it most.

***

friendship is the ultimate relationship.

cheers to all the friendships that have strengthened during shelter in place.

cheers to friendships that just sprouted recently.

cheers to estranged friendships that started up again.

cheers to all the crews out there who have been friends since before high school.

cheers to the friends who have each other's backs.

cheers to friendships who have seen it all and still choose to always ride for one another.

cheers to the friendships that kept you going if only for a season.

cheers friends. cheers.

four things you are entitled to do.

create boundaries.
ignore people that bother you.
make mistakes.
go where it feels like home.

if they leave while you change.

if they leave while you change
they weren't meant to take part
in your full metamorphosis.

***

change on you
looks like
heaven
)if heaven
had a face(
every second
you're shifting
micro
growing
diving deeper
into your own
higher self
i just hope
that mountain top
applauds for you
the way i
will always
always
always
be supporting
there there
by your side
regardless
regardless.

four everything's to tell yourself.

can't be everything for everyone.
can't complete everything in one day.
can't keep thinking everything is your fault.
everything everything is going to be alright.

***

these last six weeks and counting have been some of the toughest. even longer. for some only a few days. but it has been challenging. and you need to give yourself some grace. some encouragement. some consideration. no way can anything be done how you used to do things but you're doing it. you're doing it. and you're doing it great.

say these things to maybe help you get through that next meeting. next shift. next conversation. next trial. next test. next screen time. next walk to the fridge. next walk outside.

breathe more today than you did yesterday. take a deep deep breath and give yourself all the care you haven't felt and need. say the words. feel the words. maybe some tension will fall away. even for a bit.

this isn't normal and what you're feeling is normal. the pressure to navigate this successfully is burdensome. and you are being successful even if you think you aren't.

maybe that was love after all.

maybe that was love after all
the kind you knew how to give.
maybe it was your only way
it just wasn't enough for me.

i needed more. deserved more. but i didn't know how to ask.

***

morning prayer brought me these words. and scattered memories of
times spent. childhood and adolescence. formative years. when you
look back at the love you were given. the love you observed. it can
be hard not to justify or defend. but as a man it's important for me
to give what i needed. to pour what i wasn't. to observe and adjust
accordingly. all love isn't good love. but i have to know good love.
we all deserve good love. the best love. that deep personalized love.

five signs of a lasting friendship.

judgement never visits.
withstands good and bad moments.
always there no matter what.
ownership of when not being a good friend.
time and distance are never barriers.

you're the kind of friend that asks what someone needs before
they open their mouth to speak.

***

every friendship goes through some sort of strain but the great
ones last. no matter what.

vulnerability is a love language.
it says:

tell me more. tell me everything.
not what i want to hear. what your
soul needs to reveal. don't worry
i'll stay. i am here. i am not
going anywhere.

speak
just speak
don't hide
don't hide
unravel those words
pressed closed
)too tightly(
around your ribcage
and tell me everything
until
every shadow
has a name
every burden
takes a breath
until every
weight
loses weight
and you feel
like you
and can
finally
fly.

you deserve this kind of love.

the first they want to call.
the first they want to hug.
their very own star they wish upon.

***

you're the entire sky and everything gravity holds.

no longer accepting.

inconsistency.
bad energy.
negativity.
half-love.
excuses.

you have every right to let go whenever you want.

just know i'm tired
tired of
holding what's not mine
and have decided
to walk away
)not run(
from who and what
no longer serve me
too tired
too tired
too tired
to hold
what drains me
pains me
just know
this a'int
about you
it's time
)way past due(
to choose me
to love me
to breathe me.

balance.

we're all busy. trying to balance. whatever balance means to you. and it is a lot. the expectation to be able to handle all of this gracefully. bet if you wrote all the things you're trying to balance you'd shake your head in disbelief. you know you're holding a lot but seeing it in front of you in your own hand makes it more real. evidence that whatever you're doing is working but some stuff hasn't been watered. don't feel bad that some has been neglected. figure out what is important right now and do that.

my list was about 15 items long. big buckets. not the tasks or duties or intricacies that goes into each. each one is its own job. its own attention. you may just have one. you might have thirty. no comparison here. we're all trying.

use this time to decide what's easy and what is important. and whatever you do i know you'll rise. you. always. do.

just because.

check in on your strong friends.
the ones you think have it all together.
a simple *thinking of you*
hope you're doing okay
any worries to get off your chest
signals to even the strongest
that they too are looked after
that they too can crumble
that they too can human.

the strongest are the softest. the way they earth and sky. the way
they hold the world and let the world hold them. they need love,
too. they need love, too.

***

i may rock
but for good reason
ask me why
wonder
why
i'll tell you
i'll tell you
just ask
just ask.

love. it's not a race.

love.
it's not a race.
take it slow.
we are
icicles
clenched
on fences.
soon to be
puddles
on the ground.

ten reasons communication matters.

highest form of vulnerability that builds trust.
let's the ones you love in on how you feel.
you let go of what may be weighing you down.
increase in emotional closeness and intimacy.
avoids negative misunderstandings.
erodes the barrier of fear and isolation.
prevents and helps resolve problems.
builds deeper love and soul level connection.
signals psychological safety to say what's real.
stregthens the foundation of the relationship.

communication is hard but loving speech and openness deepens
the relationship.

***

sharing how you feel is challenging. especially if you don't feel safe
and fear what you say will bring negative consequences. but when
you lean into this work with someone you care for the relationship
can't do anything but beautifully grow.

five golden rules.

be humble.
open doors for others.
say thank you.
listen more than you speak.
share how you feel.

no matter how far or how successful or how famous you get please stay humble. no one likes to be around people who suck all the oxygen out of a room.

***

i think being a kind person is better than knowing how to solve a math problem. i think we don't know how to be generous and helpful because we think social emotional learning and skills is less important than being successful. whatever that means. i want my son to help others versus put others down. i want him to be around people who listen and don't assume what he needs. i want all of our children to be loved and appreciated. just because we had messed up childhoods and people walking in unaddressed trauma doesn't mean ours should experience the same. let's do better and ensure the generations that come after us heal and feel better and don't suffer from our mistakes.

problem solving is important don't get me wrong but how can we solve problems if we don't know how to genuinely get along.

next time your heart beats
these words will find you.

and tell you
this.

do you hear it?
keep going.
do you feel it?
the awe.

no one is you. that is your magic.
your secret reminder. tell yourself
whenever you forget.

***

you deserve all the deserves. the best. the warmest. the fullest. the
longest. the stuff you write about. and pray about. and talk about.
if you want it it's yours. it's already yours. just gotta dig for it a bit.
everyone deserves this. no one can give you what you already have.

ten still's even through hardship.

you're still here.
you're still powerful.
you're still capable.
you're still strong.
you're still wonderful.
you're still beautiful.
you're still magic.
you're still standing.
you're still lovable.
you're still you.

***

you're still lovable. always lovable. still magic. always magic. still beautiful. always beautiful. still you. always you.

if you want love to last
if you want love to grow
nine roses to consider.

take accountability.
own up to your part.
set aside your pride.
try harder than you are.
use the law of two feet
walk away if you have
to take deep breaths.
don't stand in the fire
if you're unwilling
to feel any heat.
shine light in the dark.
heal old wounds.
trust the process.

***

you have that sweet spot kind of love. it doesn't waver. it gives space for mistakes. your tough love makes diamonds.

it's okay

to be sad.
to be terrified.
to be afraid.
to be upset.
to be angry.

it's not okay

to be told to swallow your feelings because it makes others feel
bad or uncomfortable or for anyone to make you think you have
to suppress negative emotions.

take time for you. be gentle with you.

one beautiful thing you already know
but will never admit. rare ones never do.

you're inspiring. no matter if you want to
believe or breathe that in. it is true. you doubt
it because you are bashful and don't need the
recognition. you let your heart speak for
itself. modesty is your super power but deep
down you light magic firestorms in the souls
of others who desire to always be around
you. you are a grounding force. a stabilizer.
people watch and admire and soak in your
sun wondering how you are the way you are.
soft. mighty. gifted. talented. beautiful.
the universe isn't good at taking compliments.
don't be surprised how many awe over you.

you can't force someone to care.

you can't force someone to care.
or get them to see what you see.
feel how you feel. all you can do
)all you really can do(is hope
they never have to suffer what
you have to absorb constantly.
what you have to carry in your
throat and pretend it's not cutting
off your air. maybe they will never
know daytime nightmares or brutal
reminders telling them stay in their
place and don't get too comfortable.
you. beautiful resilient strong one.
will always know how to overcome.

***

you wouldn't wish hardship on anyone. not the kind that breaks
your back. you are the type that would carry their pain on top of
yours so they feel no strain.

#irunwithmaud
#ahmaudarbery
5.8.20

what everyone deserves.

to feel seen.
to be heard.
to be loved.
to be appreciated.
to be trusted.
to feel safe.
to belong.
to know joy.
to know happiness.
to find purpose.

how many times can i tell you i love you before you let it pierce your skin and drink my words like i drink your honey. never will i ever get enough of telling you the deepest truth: that i cherish you. that i love you. i love you.

***

you deserve to be to feel to know to experience all this world has to offer. all a loved one can give you. because it is you that provides all the goodness and care and attention. you deserve these giveaways like endless running water that returns back to itself.

maybe it isn't working
because it isn't meant for you
five questions to ask before you leave.

does it bring me joy?
does it drain me?
does it align with my values?
does it treat me kind?
does it require me to be someone i am not?

the old you would stay out of consideration of others. the new you leaves spaces that take you for granted.

***

not everyone should have access to you. your talents. your heart. your love. notice how you feel around people. trust your intuition. you know when you're being used and when you're being appreciated.

you can't always leave but you can let them know what isn't going to happen anymore. they've been warned.

accept. love. give. feel. repeat.

accept you can't control what others think.
love who you are no matter what.
give yourself permission to make mistakes.
feel everything deeply.
repeat after me: *i am me and that is enough.*

you are you and that is enough.

***

i love you for who you are. not just the you that has to get done
up to go out and be presentable. the you that is anxious. the you
that has quirks that are the best beauty marks. the you that is into
things no one else is. the you that always no one has seen before.
all of you is welcome. not just some of you. part of you. but the
whole of you. you can rest with me. be your self with me. find
yourself someone you can do that with and never let them go.

three qualities of a good friend.

presence. there to celebrate your wins and reflect with you about your losses. shows up without being asked to show up.
understanding. they know that life happens and you sometimes have a lot to juggle. rather than add pressure they give you space.
honesty. tell you like it is they don't sugarcoat and say what they think you want to hear. real feedback helps friends grow.

a friend is someone who holds your truths. keeps it real with you. and gently pushes you to grow into your light. that is you. a good friend. the best kind of love anyone will find.

***

friends are like plants. some need direct light and hella water. some are cool sitting in the shade. others just need attention every now and then. friends shouldn't stress you out. they should share in your life not try and take it over. a good friend adds to the quality of your life they don't diminish it. friends who last the longest are the ones who share sunlight and add nutrients into the water of one another.

when it's hard to find the right words.

throw away the idea that you have to have the right words all the time. sometimes you make things worse trying to fix what can't be fixed in the moment. so sometimes the only thing you can do is just feel. slow down. turn on music. relax in a bath. burn candles and just. sit. no need to say a word. no need to justify. no need to pinpoint. the best remedy can simply be being. that is your body telling you to come back to it. spend time with you. spend time with you.

when your body tells you to come home. listen. and your body is holy ground worthy of your attention.

***

there are no right answers. not right now. and today felt like everyone was in a frenzy. could have been the weather. could have been a reminder. for all of us to pause. to relax. to take a breath. to return to ourselves instead of always trying to be "productive" to "solve" to "create" to "do" when all we should really be doing is just "be". so if you felt a bit "off" today you aren't alone. off just means you gotta listen rather than resist. so listen. you'll know what you need.

what you deserve to hear.

i love you.
i am proud of you.
i am here for you.
i appreciate all that you do.
i apologize for hurting you.
i see how much you've grown.
i want you to be happy.
you are beautiful.
you are my person.

you are unlike anyone i've ever known. you are a refreshing
mystery not just anyone can understand. your heart)that heart(is
bold and pure. you are aurora borealis it's hard to look away and
not stay captivated.

***

if no one told you today. i love you. i'm proud of you. i am here for you. i
appreciate all that you do. i apologize for hurting you. i see how much
you've grown. i want you to be happy. you are beautiful. you are my
person. you just did. i just told you. now tell yourself. go tell someone
else. mean it. do it. pass it. breathe it. spread love. always spread love.

two definitions of insanity.

hoping a situation will change after you give chance after chance after chance and nothing ever gets better. allowing people to stand in their power by shrinking yourself so they maintain dominance and control. quit playing small because you were always meant to live big. that doesn't mean be rude or unkind. water is soft and peaceful. strong and thunderous. you are both. you can be both.

***

don't diminish yourself for the benefit of status quo. stand up for yourself. be an upstander and support those you witness being put down or disrespected. good people exist because good people don't put up with tyrants. speak truth to power and never back down for what you know is good and decent and is a human right. evil can't win because love is mightier. always mightier.

let go of

toxic relationships.
unhealthy habits.
negative self-talk.
deficit mindset.
incomplete stories.
people that gaslight you.

hold onto

what serves your spirit. what helps you move
to the next level rather than inhibit potential.
people that genuinely want to see you flow.
it's not just about staying close to people that
feel like sunlight. it's about being the light.
being who you need for yourself and others.

***

be the kind of person you want in your love story. in your hope
story. your life story. that person you can be proud of. that person
you can say wasn't making life hard for others but was paving a
path for future generations.

juneteenth is a love language.
it says:

always remember. never forget. liberation doesn't
mean free if other people are not. now is the time
to go back and get others. to shake loose chains
that bind their mind and their heart and their
hands from truly being able to see. to feel.
to understand. the bondange. the damage.
the hardship on bodies other people fear.
come and learn and celebrate and cry.
this is our history. our legacy. our task.
to recall and re-visit and remind and bring
light and love to independence. let go of not
knowing. now you know. the pain of our past
still knocks under our flag. be the change. risk.
fight. recognize we are all linked.

we still have work to do.

ten be's to hold in your heart.

be you. unapologetically all of you.
be free. do what fills your buckets.
be wonder. keep some of you to yourself.
be why. center the reasons you rise.
be lover. speak the language of love.
be persistent. continue even through difficulty.
be dreamer. go after your hearts desire.
be warrior. defend values you care about.
be happy. become the happiness you feel.
be. you'll find what you are looking for.

you are life. the below and the above. the current and could be.
you are a blessing and deserve all the good all the grace all the
favor on its way to you.

***

i hope the hint of a smile you smile today is deep. real. joyful.
that you find a gear inside you to tackle what you've been
putting on back burner. that you choose something that fills
your bucket. days have been blending but you're the being
everyone looks forward to seeing. so see today through. see
it through. see you through. you are loved. always loved.

therapy is a love language.
it says:

breathe. breathe deeper. what brings you here. what do you need.
what do you want to take a look at. how can i support you. this is a
space for you to talk out loud. feel out loud. examine those shadows.
parts of you that you ignore. parts of you that you don't know are
there. breathe. breathe some more. do you want to go there. has this
always been a true statement. the story you tell yourself. no answers
here. no judgements here. just questions. just mirrors. just you. your
full self. you don't have to tense here. you can let down here. let go
here. rest here. quiet here. cry here. anger here. release here. unwind
here. journal here. human here. stay awhile. love yourself here.

***

show up for yourself. invest in yourself. whether group or one on one. collapse into the process and trust what you find as possibility not prognosis. as information not judgement. too often we don't think it is for us but let me tell you we need it. we need it. we need it. therapy should be a free service to all. every being should have access to a culturally competent and mindful and inclusive and experienced professional to lead them back to themselves. can't heal on our own if we don't know we're in pain. chronic doesn't mean you are strong chronic means your body has kept score for way too long and you're used to feeling out of balance as normal. that isn't normal. all of you needs good care. so take care. take. care. you deserve space to unpack everything and choose what you want to focus on first. bit my bit. trust your heart.

it's okay

to not know how you feel.
to pass if you don't want to share.
to not get it right.
to be imperfect.

it's not okay

to have your worth and value tethered to sets of unrealistic standards. to be forced to know what everything means that is going on with your body and mentality. don't let someone project onto you their own insecurities. you deserve to define you. reclaim you. you are everything you need when you need you most.

***

it's okay to not be okay. it's okay to not know. it's okay to be figuring things out. it's never okay for someone to rush your process. you are everything you need when you need you most. you are everything you need when you need you most.

treat yourself kinder today. rest if you can. slow down if you can. you must. you must. don't take on someone else's stuff today you have enough to process. it's okay to request something to be done later or pushed to the side. and if they aren't understanding of what you need take that mental note)push through like you do(and do the best you can. as our favorite maya angelou once said, people will forget what you tell them but hella remember how you made them feel. always go high. they'll never clip your wings.

fifteen you don't have to's for the lover in you.

you don't have to please everyone.
you don't have to remain silent.
you don't have to pretend to care.
you don't have to bury all that pain.
you don't have to say yes if you want to say no.
you don't have to stay where you aren't happy.
you don't have to allow racism to persist.
you don't have to exist in uncertainy.
you don't have to feel guilty for not knowing.
you don't have to care what others think.
you don't have to give your energy away.
you don't have to apologize for how you feel.
you don't have to be someone you are not.
you don't have to announce your soul work.
you don't have to change your love for anyone.

can't unsee what you've seen. take what you have seen and learned and do something. don't advertise the book you read or the pdf you downloaded or the BIPOC you amplified. this isn't about short term feel goods. this is long term livelihood for the soul of our world. for human beings with targets on our backs you're just now seeing. tired yet. over it yet. done yet. imagine the everyday the generations the inheritance of the weight of a lens you can never take off. when your birth prescription was hatred fear and racism to combat like a war that just won't quit. imagine. we been tired. stay in this. you now have no choice to go back to when you didn't know. be on the right side this time. neutral or indifference is just as detrimental. act and force others off the fence.

expectations to remove from your mind.

not everyone is going to love the way you do.
not everyone will give the way you give.
not everyone can come where you are going.
not everyone should have access to your heart.
not everyone is as mindful as you are.
not everyone has patience to wait like you.
not everyone can light up a room like you.
not everyone will understand your decisions.
not everyone makes love deep enough for you.

you are deserving of a world that doesn't exist yet. to taste flavors of a love filled with ingredients that nourish you. but no one loves or gives or provides like you. nobody nobody. but there are some who will blow your mind if you give them a chance. you are hard to satisfy. how does one fill an already full moon.

***

you are the words wow in motion. but if you can let go of so many expectations it may just open up a whole new experience versus trying to control the outcome. they say expectation is a thief of joy and that has truth but you should know there are some expectations that are non-negotiable like. being around decent people who treat you right. wanting to feel special because you are. and people having the decency to be good human beings. not too hard to ask but sadly hard to come by. grateful people like you exist. reminds other humans to do better. i hope they lead by your loving example. until then. keep living and being a beacon for those that can't see and be as bright as you. we need you.

the best kind of hugs.

you don't know this. or maybe you do. but hugs from you breathe new life. hugs from you soften the hardship someone is going through. the best kind of hugs do that. they with open arms are free of questions just full of *i know* and *i'm here* and *i love you.* you are everyone's favorite hug. their go-to comfort love. they fall into you and body feels body and mind calms down. soul shifts and sighs and sobs and sorrows from long days vanish in your embrace. when all of this is over they will come to you. they will reach for you. and you will heal and give how you heal and give best. deep deep hugs.

hugs from you heal. hugs from you are the richest prayer. a gift wrapped in skin. what a healer you are. what a healer you are.

you are entitled to say no.

you are entitled to say no
and not justify reasons why.

***

no is a full sentence. you don't have to convince someone as to why. they are already trying to persuade you to change your mind.

what to tell your inner self-critic.

leave me alone.
you're holding me back.

you belong. you are strong. you're meant to be where you are.
without you there is a void no one could ever ever fill.

***

tell that inner self-critic to go. turn that negative voice down. turn
your light hella loud and up.

when someone you love asks

what are you doing?
are you busy?
you good?
can you talk?

they are really saying

i miss you.
i feel disconnected.
i'm worried about you.
i don't want anything
from you. i just want
you to know i'm
thinking of you.

your kind of care is rare. every soul who knows you knows you is
damn lucky to know you know you. so many crave your attention.
but you don't even know why people think you're special. can you
see why now. you're adorably down to earth.

***

simple as it sounds you make friendship feel like a cruise. all
you can eat. dope entertainment. open 24/7. everything you'd
want to do. it's like you read minds and stock up knowing what
loved ones need before they approach you. that is you. always
ready. always ready. and when you connect hours can go by
and it's hard to go back away from you. what an elixir you are.

no longer avoid.

your past.
your pain.
your problems.

tend to your healing.
give yourself grace.
wounds don't vanish
by throwing yourself
under a rug.

you can't find yourself if you hide from yourself. stop running. you will be okay. you are lovely as you are. you are loved because you are.

***

all of us deal with something. one day or another. today or tomorrow. from the past. from the past. struggle and worry and anxious and run away from and in denial of. no one is exempt. no one. so don't think you are on an island when all of us are right there next to you. doubting. worrying. wondering. frightened. impostering. hurting. avoiding. but if we just lean in and choose one thing to focus on. one issue to tackle in ourselves. not to perfect but to love on and be there. not run from or posture. we will collectively heal. we will move back in towards ourselves instead of moving out and wounding others. you got this because we got this. together. this isn't a battle of who has the most trauma. this is a war for our collective soul. may we help one another by being vulnerable and kind.

where their attention should have been.

funny how they pay attention to you
when you remove attention from them
and focus it on where their attention
should have been. on you.

***

the most beautiful i miss you
without saying i miss you.

this song hit different today and i thought of you.
it's been too long since i felt your beautiful soul.
when are you available to connect. i've been
waiting all day to see your name pop up on my
phone. you're my favorite favorite. just calling
to hear your voice. do you remember the time
we stayed up all night. where have you been
all my life. think you'd like this movie.
just saying hi. can you fill me in. read this.
tell me what you think. i love you. xo.

what love is.

a safe place.
a growth zone.
a homecoming.

it isn't always
pretty or tied with
a bow. it often has
countless knots to
untangle. loose ends
to discover. maybe
love is about finding
the people who are
willing to persist.
wanting you for you.

***

you are an unfound love. an untapped stream. love from you is
discovering new land never occupied or conquered or tarnished.
protect your love as much as possible. it isn't selfish to love your
love. it is selfish of you not to love your love.

giving is a love language.
it says:

this isn't about me. this is about you. for you.
centering and focusing your needs and desires
and joys is what brings me to life. providing
space and time and energy is like water for soul.
love for heart. air for lungs. share how i can give you
what i have all i have when i have because it's yours.
it's always been yours. tell me how i can support and
take any undue load you are carrying. you are special
to me. i see and sense you. i want to forever see your
light burn bright.

***

everyone you give to has experienced deep love. genuine love. some can't handle it. some didn't know what to do with it. some so badly look forward to it. regardless you keep giving because you are you. stay you. keep you even if they expect you to be someone else. the giver in me honors the giver in you.

accountability is a love language.
it says:

i know this is hard. to take ownership.
to avoid making mistakes. to stand in the fire.
but i need you. to be honest. to not just talk
about changing behaviors and noticing
patterns. but to really do the work. to show
you want this. want us. to thrive and always
be in bloom. yes it will get hot. scorching
at times. but i'll never treat you cold and leave
you on the side of the road. trust me. i got you.
i have you. more than you know. let go of that
fear to be truthful. i'm here for you. i love you.

four clear signs a boundary has been set.

they stop responding.
conversations get shorter.
they tell you straight up: *please stop.*
the energy dramatically shifts.

boundaries are a love language. when you set them and articulate what you aren't about and what you are for watch who stays and see who flees.

***

it's okay to say no and it's okay to literally unfollow unhealthy situations be it on social media or in real life. sometimes it isn't that easy to walk away so quickly but you can arrange for what needs to happen for you to stay safe and sane or make plans to leave momentarily.

few are taught what boundaries are and many are taught that boundaries don't matter. that they can do as they please and get away with violating others. a lot of unlearning has to happen.

you are the master of your own body. the captain of your energy. who you give you to is all up to you.

three insecurities to break up with.

not being good enough. the biggest lie. so far from the truth. you have always been good enough. your enough is just too much for people who aren't prepared for a soul like yours.
not fitting in. you were not made to fit in. you were made to stand out. don't give up parts of yourself in exchange for false love.
the real you wouldn't be accepted. all of you is authentic. genuine. if you have to front and be someone else around people then those are not your people.

if they are gentle with what you are insecure about then they will remind you that you have nothing to worry about. if they can't love you for you then they aren't meant for you. period.

insecurities show up daily. in all of us. with how we look. what we wear. how we show up. what we can and can't do so not to come off a certain way to maintain being acceptable. if that sounds exhausting it's because it is exhausting. can't wear all those masks at once. your skin is your skin. your heart is your heart. everyone has stuff to work on but no one should ever intentionally make you feel worthless or less than magic. so pick yourself up on those days someone)even you(presses into where you don't feel confidently you. you're human. your brain can play tricks on you. just know it will be okay. it will be okay. stay close to people who remind you of your light. stand in front of the mirror and tell yourself how incredible you are. mirrors aren't glass. you aren't made of glass. so stand in front of yourself and talk that love talk. fill others with your good love. and break up with feelings of not being good enough and not fitting in and thinking the real you wouldn't be accepted. watch how you move differently after those relationships wither.

nine reasons you're afraid to love.

because of old wounds.
because of old experiences.
because of old pain.
because of old broken promises.
because of old unhappiness.
because of old lies.
because of old immature lovers.
because of old fears.
because of old stories about your worth.

***

you're not just letting anyone in. you're cautious. it's okay to be cautious. great pyramids aren't built just for anyone. you're entitled to decide who you allow in your temple.

what you want to do

reach out to an ex.
talk to someone already involved.
pretend everything is okay.
dodge difficult conversations.

what you should do

focus on yourself.
respect boundaries.
water your own relationship.
ask yourself why.

***

you can't force water to go where it doesn't want to flow but you
can flow with it and see where you end up. if they can't be patient
and want to rush that already tells you what you need to know.

no longer accepting. II

temporary love.
temporary support.
temporary allyship.
temporary promises.
temporary respect.
temporary solutions.
temporary connection.
temporary vulnerability.
temporary honesty.
temporary presence.

***

you are that long-term love. that forever always infinity kind of love. the keep you up wondering if you're still up kind of love. nothing temporary about you.

the most beautiful i love you
without saying i love you.

saw this and thought of you.
you do so much for me.
saying goodbye is always hard.
you're my forever mood.
you complete all of me that was missing.
meeting you healed me.
you have the most beautiful heart.
you make me better and don't even know it.

***

you are the rarest wonder. love from you has no end only countless mysteries that drop into beautiful abyss. saying i love you to someone like you doesn't even hold a candle to a lover like you who knows no limit and drowns the deepest oceans.

you deserve to live a full life.

you deserve to live a full life. the fullest life. but they fear you. the thought of you. the sight of you. the hue of you. the magic in you. the crown in you. the god in you. your life will aways be a threat to those who hate themselves.

***

you don't deserve an outrage post or a side chair activist or twenty seconds of i can't believe this happened. you deserve action. a phone call to someone who knows someone who can hear the cries we've been crying. stop killing us with your guilt and shame and inaction and post racial ideology. covid is ripping us just like trees on southern plantations. are you still reading or did your repost earlier exceed your one protest a decade to support hit your quota. this isn't an angry letter this is a where have you been dilemma. we're tired of telling you we can't breathe cause you still don't believe you're at our throats even if our knees have cleats that so called disrespect a flag. how many names can you recite. how many hashtags do you know of people that look like you that were slain on and off camera at the hands of someone that look like you who just say they feared for their life and got off because history teaches you that your fear overrules. how many names have you come up with yet. how often are you reminded of your place because of your race that tells you stay in your place cuz your place will make it repeatedly on every news outlet on repeat to re-open a wound to tell unborn children that free means you can't run. that free means not really. that free means just barely. how many names have you dug up. the trauma the trauma. can't even bury our own before they throw another one on top of the other one. #breonnataylor

when someone says

i can't breathe.
my stomach hurts.
my neck hurts.
everything hurts.

they are telling you

i can't breathe.
get off.
help me.
you're killing me.

***

hate is heavy. but there is so much money in hate. it feeds and divides. hate controls and dictates. but love cuts through hate like a knife. this is why they don't want to teach you how to love. for love dismantles who they think they are. #georgefloyd

five self-care tips to navigate traumatic events.

affinity group. it is okay to gather in safety with those similar to you to process and unpack and grieve and resource and breathe and silence and feel without having to apologize for being triggered and hurt. it is not your job to educate others while trying to rehab your own wounds. checking in with community is a natural reaction to heal.

make art/tap into art. read. write. listen. sing. respond. art is therapy. it releases what typically gets trapped in the body and gets rid of some of all that built up tension. it says feel.

do nothing. take time to collect your inner peace.

unplug. get off the social grid. protect your pyschic energy. logging in and seeing replay and repost after repost further initiates being activated and re-traumatized. unplugging can control what you let in. give yourself permission to log off.

feel. your reaction is your reaction. do not apologize if rage visits quicker than patience allows. you have every right to be tired an angry and frustrated and terrified and sad and scared and numb. the problem is you aren't allowed to rage. rage if you must. for some rage is a constant state. let rage visit but do not stay there. share your emotions.

four ways to show up for traumatized people.

disrupt hate. see something say something. be a good human being. you can't wait to be directly impacted until you decide to fight for your fellow human being. respond to what your inner circle says and push back on them and your internal dialogue. you know what you say and do.

do your work. people who have experienced systemic oppression are not responsible to teach you how to end it or tell you what to do to feel better. read books. search how to be an ally. sign up and attend conferences. do not seek out someone who is close in proximity to the pain. underrepresented people's backs have been stood on for far too long.

check-in on historically marginalized peoples. you watch and listen to the news. you know what is going on. a simple check-in goes a long way. it says you care. that you are here. don't offer solution. offer fellowship. don't assume. just ask.

stop making excuses. saying you don't know what you can do is no longer acceptable. everyone can do something. it's just a matter of choice. stop engaging with overtly hateful people. stop endorsing certain campaigns. invest differently. doing nothing means you are complicit to systems of hate.

when you don't know what to say
say something anyway. dozen roses
to send someone you care about.

just checking in. you don't have to respond. there is a lot going on and you are on my mind. if you ever want to talk know that you can reach out to me. day or night. right now. 2am. i don't know how you are feeling but i'm down to hold some of that for you. hold you in ways you need when you feel no one is there. but i care. i'm no good with words but actions speak louder. i apologize for saying nothing sooner. charge it to my head and not my heart. how are you. give me your burdens. you have me always. thinking of you always. i love you.

***

uncried tears still cry. just come out in different forms. you deserve someone to say something before you have to. you deserve a tribe of loved ones who can sense a change of your wind because they know the temperature of you. how can someone say they know you if they don't know what you care about. what rattles you. what drives you. sometimes they don't reach for lack of words but no excuse to say nothing or do nothing at all. it's not on you to make someone care. if they cared they'd find a way. if it was them feeling down they know what it's like to be held and picked up. don't force anymore. don't do it. just notice who is there while the dust and fog and tunnel is present and who are the ones blocking the water and the light and saying what about me what about me. move away from people who in your soul know aren't good for you anymore.

a random letter you should write somebody.

you. oh you. if you could see through me you'd see i'm 2% me and 98% filled of you. you occupy all of me. every word i recite is yours. may you know the love you unselfishly share is the water i'm entirely made of.

***

the most beautiful hello
without saying hello.

finally.
there you are.
nice seeing you.
can't believe this.
where have you been.
my heart is beating fast.
you were just on my mind.
tell me we us will last forever.
be still my body speaks your name.
embracing you is my love language.
can we just stare and say nothing at all.

four types of love you need.

physical love. touch. closeness. presence.
mental love. understanding. thought provoking.
emotional love. feeling seen. connected. wanted.
spiritual love. chemistry. energy. meaningful.

go where this is fostered and grown.
leave where this is nowhere to be found.
you deserve to be flooded with love
not searching for dried up wells.

***

make that decision you been holding yourself back from. you
know what you have to do.

what you didn't know
you needed to hear.
seven soul reminders.

do not apologize for your rage.
do not apologize for your grief.
do not apologize for your helplessness.
do not apologize for your body.
do not apologize for your withdrawal.
do not apologize for your healing.
do not apologize for your tears.

the lover in you is engaging in vulnerability.
you are allowed to feel and make no apology
and know that you are loved. love. it never
neglects. it holds. it holds. holding you still.

***

learning to notice when i am holding myself too tight and not
wanting anyone else near me. learning to read each goosebump
as news telling me i need warmth or that you're nearby. learning
to remember that grief has no timeline. that grief is personal.
that grief shows up in happy times. times your mind is engaged
in joy and then can get stripped away unexpectedly. learning to
breathe underwater with my mouth wide open to fill back up
when i feel depleted. learning to stop comparing myself to the
last time grief paid visit. learning that being human is by nature
vulnerable. and running from being vulnerable means running
from myself. so i beg you to learn to embrace grief when it
comes. in whatever stage. to catch it and name it and don't
apologize for emotions that needs to come out and be released.

right now and always.

you are crucial.
you are important.
you are necessary.
you are worthy.
you are powerful.
you are soft.
you are strong.
you are supported.
you are growing.
you are blooming.
you are beautiful.
you are magic.
you are significant.

fifteen powers in your control.

the power to prioritize mental health.
the power to set boundaries.
the power to walk away.
the power to say no this isn't right.
the power to think for yourself.
the power to unfollow people in real life.
the power to challenge positional power.
the power to make change.
the power to love unconditionally.
the power to speak your truth.
the power to spread positivity.
the power to address new and old wounds.
the power to lean into discomfort.
the power to stand up for what you believe in.
the power to make mistakes and learn from them.

you have this power about you. this mighty about you. this beautiful gentleness and this fierceness about you. let no one ever think they can take that away.

***

take a mental health day. take multiple. spread them out. take them all at once. this is your life and your body and your body and your body and your body. it's okay to water yourself by removing yourself out from up under heaviness and the busy and the too much. even if for just some hours or some days. some of us have been unable to break away even if breaks were taken. some of us have been on break since always. some of us know what it's like to slowly be breaking. some of us break and never return the same. protect your mental health.

protesting is a love language.
it says:

i am not being heard. you are not listening.
change needs to be made. repair must be done.
don't you see i am hurt. historical pain. i can't
do this anymore. the waiting. the being unseen.
these signs. these screams. this boiling. is my
right to object to disapprove to stand. no more.
no more. open your eyes and your heart. you
will respect me. by any means. hear my roar.

***

you deserve more. more peace. more love. more respect. more attention. more understanding. more effort. more protection. you can't keep thinking you'll get anything from a deserted heart. a vacant love. an empty relationship. they will live in regret every day once you leave. you deserve more. more better. so much better.

you matter. so much. so much. without you every fire would be snow and every star would be sad and fall out of the sky. you are what hope turns to when people sit and manifest. you are dusk and dawn and the beautiful hues in between. you. you. are the color purple before and after midnight. the natural world always aligns itself to your moon phase your calendar your breath your infinity magic. you beloved. you matter. no matter how many try to deny your legendary presence.

ten no more's moving forward.

no more shrinking yourself.
no more settling for less than you deserve.
no more holding what what you feel.
no more putting yourself on the back burner.
no more letting their shadow frighten you.
no more making the same mistakes.
no more code switching for their approval.
no more falling into hold unhealthy patterns.
no more situations that don't help you grow.
no more being someone you aren't for others.

***

you are your own super power. your own hero. your own knight.
you are the one. but you can't always be the default to do the work
for others. to do your work and theirs. that is unfair and should stop.
you can't tend to your wounds and the guilty wounds of the one
who pained you. fixing you doesn't mean it gives others permission
to pile on their own stuff because you're already doing it. fixing
you means you know yourself best to know when you need to shed
parts that have been holding on to you that need to be removed.

when the fires stop and the smoke clears.

everything you do won't please everyone.
anything you do will potentially offend and
unintentionally strike a chord in someone.
if this happens. when this happens. wonder
for a moment why you did or said or cried
or pleaded. wonder where your heart was.
then stand like oak and root. root. root. root.
tall and firm. fist beating like the beautiful
organ beneath your skin held in ribcage.
let their response or their withdrawal or
unfollow or attack or passiveness not
deter or unravel your resolve. your
good will outweigh the darkness.
you are dismantling. your heat
is too hot for them anyway.

your heat is too hot for them anyway. so when they run off they were never really there in the first place. for when you dismantle you dissolve and puncture a foundation others built on backs who truly know what heat feels like. you can't let others stop what burns inside you because they don't want to be uncomfortable or burn. that tells you you're on to something. something they have always been scared of. everything you do won't please everyone. but the time is now to stop playing politics and start living in reality. go with your gut. places are burning and you're yearning to say or do something because you see the fires and the smoke. but what will you do when all that clears. will you still have that fight in you. that ore in you. that flame that says we can't let up. or will you fizzle because those close to you go back to business as usual. be the one that stands in with those who need to be stood with. don't find yourself lost in a crowd of people who stand for nothing.

allyship is a love language.
it says:

tell me what you need. i don't know what to do or what to say
but i am here. at the ready. willing. no criticism. no judgement.
if you tell me to do nothing i will do nothing. if you tell me to speak
i will lift my voice even if the wrong things come out. no more will i
be idle. no more will i watch you suffer. i am with you. here to listen.
here to fight. here to shoulder and make up for battles i have missed.
i may be late but that won't happen again. standing. holding.
bleeding. mobilizing. unpacking my own biases. my own privilege.
full-time. i will learn. unlearn. disrupt systems of power.
if you will have me. or not. i'm doing the work.

***

you can't just call yourself an ally. one must bestow that term upon you. in the meantime you can do the work. you can check your blindspots and your implicit biases and your prejudice and your privilege. too many people say they are allies but don't show up. they stand behind a term only using it when it works for their schedule. but an ally)a true ally(is that ride or die. that person who will get you at 2am even if they were too tired but show up for you anyway because they care about your safety. a true ally gives up some of their power/resources/platform to genuinely spread awareness not just to check a box. want to be an ally? learn about the issues. don't seek a person who is fighting for their rights to teach you about that experience. that is the worst thing you could do. the best thing you can do is open your eyes. attend events someone you know is promoting. go. bring a friend. listen. do not interrupt. be open. then show up to the next one. and to the fundraiser. and to the rally. and to the canvasing. and to the telephones to spread more information about what the fight is really all about. don't just change your social media profile photo. don't just share a few posts written by people impacted by the fight itself. unlearn. interrupt the terrible racist, sexist, homophobic, transphobic, xenophobic, all the -ists and -phobics and offensive jokes/parties/comments/remarks people in your circle make. don't make excuses in saying you don't know what else to do. to be an ally isn't a part-time gig. do the work or you'll forever be part of the problem.

six types of courage you need.

moral courage. to do the right thing.
emotional courage. to heal your wounds.
spiritual courage. to trust the process.
physical courage. to brave the unknown.
social courage. to be your authentic self.
intellectual courage. to learn and unlearn.

it takes great strength to do something or face
someone that frightens you. to move even though
you just want to stay still. honor all that courage.
stop being so hard on yourself. you're human.

you are courage in fire and should be proud of where you are
based off of all the difficulty you have souled through. hearted
through. toughed through. you are a goddamn warrior.

james baldwin once said: not everything that is faced can be
changed but nothing can be changed until it is faced. keep facing
and addressing and fighting and working through and figuring
out. no matter what happens you can say you gave it your all.

you are a love language.
that says:

see me. love me. want me. honor me. accept me.
cherish me. embrace me. acknowledge me. listen.
i am not just anyone you can walk over. anyone
to control. anyone to manipulate. come to me
respectfully. anything that isn't soaked in love
i don't want near me. don't bring non-love unlove
counterfeit love or empty love. unless you are
willing to be capsized. willing to be raptured and
covered with my kind of love. whole and deep.
bottomless. if you aren't ready stay away.
love costs here. costs vulnerability. costs trust.
costs commitment. costs accountability. costs
maturity. to love me you must hold your breath
and be ready for the best love of your lifetime.

***

you deserve nourishing love. the kind you nourish others with.
you deserve deep love. the kind you deep others with. you deserve
sunny love. the kind you sun others with. but not everyone is you
and it can feel like looking for love in hopeless places. but it's there
when you stop looking. the kind that fills everything you are. be the
love of your life.

gratitude is a love language.
it says:

thank you. not in quick passing but in deep
reflection. i may not say it out loud or even
show my appreciation. for your work. for
all that you do. for the unseen. the unvalidated.
the invisible toil. the thankless things you do.
always. i see you. i hear you. i feel you. i love
you. evergrateful and that doesn't begin to
address what you have done for me. in times
i just wanted to give in and give up and quit.
you stayed. you were a light. always a light.
guiding. lifting. bringing you to my attention
is past due. i need to tell you this more often.
you don't have to say anything back. thank you.
you are what i cherish most. grateful you exist.

when someone asks

are you anti-racist.
do black lives matter.
what are you unlearning.

what they want to know is

do you care. will they be safe with you. is your response authentic.
your level of discomfort. if you are worthy of their time and energy.
no one is perfect and change doesn't happen overnight. but if you
get defensive)that is normal(that is for you to work through. no
one is calling you out they are calling you in. all that frustration and
embarrassment or guilt or shame or indifference is information for
you to navigate. do your work.

***

we all have work to do. all of us. if a question or a statement
offends you ask yourself why. take the time to really examine it.
don miguel ruiz reminds us of the four agreements and one is to
not take things personally. although hard it is a game changer. to
not take it personal. to see the words and actions of others as a
gift to see if your actions align with your words. you would want
someone to ensure you are safe and that you belong and that your
family and loved ones have nothing to worry about. take a breath
before you respond to questions and that will make a whole world
of difference. do good. do better.

what to keep

your heart.
your compassion.
your resilience.
your humanity.

what to leave behind

all that hate. all that misunderstanding.
all that prejudice. all that mistreatment.
how: check your bias. check your soul.
love deeper. see the beauty in others.

***

this place. these people. our world. isn't perfect. our own households
have challenge and difficulties. but come on. in this life why can't we
make and bring ease. for all. for everyone. not just reserved for some.
you have the ability to enact change. in the microdecisions. in the
every day. in the folks you surround. don't put up with bigotry. call
hate out. leave people who use you perpetually. the shift is palpable.
give them one breath to change on the side of good and let your feet
tell them you mean business. sometimes people just don't know until
you ask them: what kind of pain are you in. why are you taking it out
on others. i love you. i'm just curious. but this is no longer behavior
i can let slide. we are all in pain but don't ruin someone else's life
because yours isn't going how you planned. and send with love.

you are what you've always been looking for and more. so much fucking more. stop looking for what you already are in others. and be who you are for yourself. *xo. adrian michael*

i appreciate you 🌹